Claims

Also by Shirley Kaufman

The Floor Keeps Turning
1969 United States Award of the International Poetry Forum and National Council on the Arts Selection

Gold Country

Looking at Henry Moore's Elephant Skull Etchings in Jerusalem During the War

From One Life to Another

Translations

My Little Sister, translated from the Hebrew of Abba Kovner. In *Abba Kovner and Nelly Sachs: Selected Poems*.

A Canopy in the Desert, translated from the Hebrew of Abba Kovner.

The Light of Lost Suns, translated from the Hebrew of Amir Gilboa.

CLAIMS

A Poem by Shirley Kaufman

The Sheep Meadow Press
New York

Acknowledgements

I wish to thank the editors of the following magazines where these poems have appeared, sometimes under different titles: *American Poetry Review, Barnwood, The California Quarterly, Crosscurrents, European Judaism, Field, The Iowa Review, Ironwood, Kayak, The Literary Quarterly, The Massachusetts Review, Midstream, The Nation, The Ohio Review, Pequod, Ploughshares, Poetry Northwest, The Virginia Quarterly Review,* and *Stand.*

"Like fear", "Brest Litovsk", "All the way back", "The distance", and "After so little" also appear in earlier versions in *Extended Outlooks,* Collier Books (Macmillan), 1982.

"Déjà vu" appears in the *Longman Anthology of Contemporary American Poetry 1950–1980,* Longman, 1983.

Grateful acknowledgement is made to the National Endowment for the Arts for a Fellowship grant in 1980-1981 while I was working on this book.

Typesetting by Keystrokes, Lenox, Mass.
Printed in the United States of America
The Sheep Meadow Press, New York, N.Y.
Distributed by Persea Books
225 Lafayette St., New York, N.Y. 10012

Library of Congress Cataloging in Publication Data

Kaufman, Shirley.
   Claims.

   I. Title.
PS3561.A862C56   1984   811'.54   84-2146
ISBN 0-935296-53-0
ISBN 0-935296-54-9 (pbk.)

For my daughters:
Sharon, Joan, and Deborah

Tan ala, tan salida, tan amor
So much wing, so much departure, so much love

César Vallejo

Table of Contents

Prologue: Jacaranda

Prologue: Jacaranda

Because the branches hang down with blossoms
for only a few weeks, lavender clumps
that let go quickly
and drop to the ground,

because the flowers are so delicate
even their motion through the air
bruises them,
and they lie where they fall
like tiny pouches of shriveled skin,

because our lives are sagging with marvels
ready to fail us,
clusters of faces drifting away,

what's settled for is not nearly
what we are after, claims
we keep making or are made on us.
But the recurrence of change
can still surprise us, lilac
that darts and flickers
like the iridescent head of a fly,
and the tree making us
look again.

I
Two Directions

1   On the way to Moriah

Next to the U.N. compound
on the Hill of Evil Counsel
where Abraham camped with Isaac
on their way to Moriah,
Burt has his business.

The path the sun makes each day
in its blind circle
hasn't changed. Except that the sky
has less space below.

Gift shop and restaurant and goat—hair tents
like a leftover outpost,
biblical shepherds still
combing the insects from their beards
or stepping on thorns between the rocks.

He explains about the Bedouin
as they serve tea with wild sage,
play the rebaba,
and the busloads of tourists
sit on old rugs and think this is it.

The Bedouin show the women
how to dance. They help them
onto the camels and everyone
smiles for the cameras.

The approximate Sinai. Dust
ripples over dust in the white heat
and the animals sway with their loads
in a stately boredom
breathing across the desert to the south.

Authentic as anything
in this improbable world.

2   The Mount of Olives

The hills slide eastward into the desert
from the Mount of Olives,
a slow process the natives ignore.
The coffee is sweet and bitter
in the small cups.

What are you doing in Jerusalem?

A donkey staggers over the slope
of the cemetery, carrying a load of rocks.
Everything glitters.
Everything's hammered by the sun
into bright mica.

Only the dead are dull.
They have all the answers.

It's a clear day. When I turn
I can see the mountains of Moab
renewing themselves in the blue distance
on the other side.

The Dead Sea shines at the bottom of the world
like the black, original water.

3   Reasons

Keep trying to tell them why I am here
but none of it's true:
fabric I cling to
the way a child drags her torn blanket
in the dark.

And the stray cats mew between my ankles
as if they remembered me.

We know what we want
before we know who we are.

That's why the angels
go up and down the ladder all night
with our petitions.

That's why a woman
opens her legs
with her eyes closed.

That's why I came down
out of the air, unsure
as each of us in the first
departure, everyone telling me
this is home.

4

This is a city of exiles.
In spring the wind lifts from the surface
of the Dead Sea over the wilderness
in a blast of sand.

It blows on the carpets as we beat them
until the threads are raw
and fall apart from each other.

All day we hear the shutters
trying to hang on, grinding
their teeth between the slats.

It blows on the ones who arrive
and the ones who leave.
The dust never settles
from so much coming and going.

5   Like fear

The guard in front of the mayor's house
walks back and forth, only a few steps
in either direction where the shade
from the jacaranda stops
in a river of light.
He keeps his feet dry.

Two stories up on Rashba
I'm at the window with the whole sky
bulging across the sill.

Not in the living–room
where no one lived, Seattle
Victorian, untouchable doilies,
dark oak smelling of polish, and the sun
stopped back of the curtains
so the upholstery wouldn't fade.

Not in the kitchen where the fat
was skimmed off the soup
like fear left over
from the first life.

6   Brest Litovsk

My mother remembered how she sat
in the cart beside her father
when he rode through the lands
of the absent landlord collecting the rents.

It was near Brest Litovsk,
the names kept changing and the peasants
would stare at them and pay.

Peasant to grandfather, Jew to Pole
each greasing the other,
steps that went nowhere
like the road to the border.

When the Cossacks came charging through the town
they bolted the doors and windows
and hid under the beds. They put pillows
over the children's mouths
to stop their cries.

There was no summer in this landscape,
even the language disappeared.
Fifty years later all she remembered
was her father's white shirt,
that he was always clean.

7   The distance

Pillows of goose down,
snow in the winter

where my mother walked
in the ditches of sorrow,
thick braids splashing between her shoulders,

or sat by the lamp they lit early
while the young man read Pushkin
leaning against her knees.

It rained in Seattle even in June.
She made fine stitches in her sheets
and waited. French knots and gossip.
The distance between them
was a hole through the center of the world
the rain kept filling. The rain
made a river in her ribs
on which her sad heart drifted.

There are words that can't travel,
threads that have lost their way home.

8   All the way back

Look at the map.
If you lose the scale
there's no way to measure
how far you have travelled
from there to here.

I roll out the strudel
as she taught me, pulling the dough
until it's thin enough to see through
all the way back.

Strangers open the door. They show me
into the room I slept in
next to my parents,
somebody else's crib, the wallpaper new
where I slipped my fingers under the seam
and tore the roses.

Sometimes I'd hear
her whimper in bed
or was it some immoderate
noise that made me
cry I'm afraid of the dark
till he stamped in the doorway
and switched on the light.

9   Honey

Fridays my father came home
for the weekend smelling of damp wool.

He knew there were things more lavish
than his Morris chair, but he sank into it
loosening his tie, and letting me
smooth the fur of his eyebrows
with my doll's comb.

He told me his mother put honey
on his tongue the first day at *heder*
to sweeten his whole life.

Peddlers dragging the dry goods
in their sacks: how much did they carry
from Ulanov over the toll bridge
to anywhere else?

Or in a suitcase. What else
could he do with his sweet talk,
8 by 10 photos of early American
pseudocolonial imitation maple beds?

Weeks when the doors kept slamming
and nothing would sell.
It rained in Eugene and Portland.
It rained in Spokane. And the sky
in Seattle would never turn off.

He said there was a restaurant
in Pocatello where the food moved
on a conveyor belt past his table
while he ate as much as he pleased.

Trickle of honey
in the one–night towns.

When he kissed my mother
her mouth was closed.

It wasn't like paradise, the first place
where we huddled together
lighting the birthday candles,
catching the rain in the attic,
or stood on a bench
extending our wings as far
as our fingers, and fell
on the floor.

Home we keep saying, the keys in our pocket,
as if there's a refuge
nothing can change.

How the same rooms console us briefly
when we return, the bed
and the table with its lamp.
The heaven of small lit porches
when the sun goes down.

A big fly lurches from window
to window in my room, crazy
for anything out there.

11   Puget Sound

North of Seattle, the Sound dwindles
into straits and the boat slows down.
The sky thickens with gulls.
They flap in my eyes and swoop
into the drifting garbage.

Islands keep pushing closer, green,
in great pelts, repeating themselves.
So I return again
to low tide and the salt smell
and a last squall of crimson before dark.
They back off.

But the small child won't let go.
She wades on her shadow
as it puckers like an old face,
looking for agates in the sand.

Come in, come in, your lips are blue!

Her white toes out of the shallow
water, puffy and wrinkled, still
running, running, up the beach.

Aunt Fan in a pleated skirt
won't take her medicine or eat.
She keeps her slippers on all day
over her sagging stockings,
dabbing "White Shoulders" behind her ears
as if Vronsky were coming.

She doesn't belong in Seattle,
no one is good enough, the first
one still follows her
home from school.

She wants me to know it.
She wants me to see her
loosen her raisin–colored hair.
She wants me to climb with her backwards
into deserted dachas,
to lie down on the damp boards,
plaster crumbling around her
as he unbuttons her blouse.

His face is fuzzy in the dim light
but I feel his hands.

13   The winning of the West

Nights when their faces press hard
at the windows and their scalps shine
pink and almost transparent
under the thin hair, their breath
makes thumbprints on the glass.

Grandpa sucks on a cube
of sugar, sipping his tea.

They are all in the kitchen
with their new names,
stirring the rusty language,
spilling it into their saucers
to let it cool.

Steam rises like dust from their bodies.

My grandmother fell down the stairs
and broke her hip. She died
in a Catholic hospital, as far
from the Czar as she could get
without crossing another ocean,
nailed through the bone.

Her wig's on the night stand,
stiff little nest
the birds have abandoned.

14

Losses. Nothing I think of
will add up to theirs, will add up
to nothing at all. There is
no equivalent for silence,
no silence thick as the bundles
around their ankles, no
place to return to.

My father sat on the toilet
reading; my mother kept talking
through the door.

If you think of the worst
that can happen, he said, you won't
be afraid.

15   Proximities

The body nurses its loud hurt
quietly. My grandfather bought
a piece of land in Palestine
he never saw. Next to
the opera house, they told him,
in Afula, after Jerusalem
the only probable paradise on earth.

And while he coughed
and knew why he coughed,
his lungs filling up
with water, grandpa
planted carrots in his backyard
next to the convent on the corner
where the nuns were hanging out
their immaculate wash.

Is it time? Is it time?
The sweet crop swelling
and the failing heart.

I pulled them up by their green hair,
small as his finger wagging *no,*
before they were ready.

16   The road out of Poland

A child who listens behind the door
to trouble, trouble.

Didn't they keep it
to themselves? All night
the road out of Poland
and all day the rain.

Ashamed of the language
like hand—me—down sweaters
the rich cousin gives
when you want something new.

The immigrant dustbin.
You shake out the past
as you shake out the cloth after dinner,
but your tongue is under the window
catching the crumbs.

17

This tongue, this mouth,
this bite they corrected, what
were they doing until now?

Another implacable language
I haven't learned. I swallow
the hook and the gutturals
catch in my throat.
The vowels are missing.

But everyone's talking. All the words
whispered into Solomon's ear.
The bird flies into the tree again,
small wings of an ancient longing.
Here.

18   **Arches**

The driver on the Egged bus closes
the door on my arm while everyone's
pushing to get in.

Half the world leans
on the other half,
to keep it firm.

The afflicted with their worn eyes
and soft bellies crowding
the hospital benches, lift
their heads as a door opens,
waiting for anyone
to give them back their names.

They lean, they lean
as the Patriarch leans
to the chalk—faced infant
at the midnight Mass
while the incense sweetens his fingers.

And an Arab woman walks
down the Street of the Chain,
a basket of figs on her head,
her back so straight she could
hold up anything, even
the lid of heaven.

19   The dome

Stressed essentials. So nothing
collapses from its own weakness.
As in the Duomo.
Brunelleschi dreamed his miracle
out of an egg.

Or the Dome of the Rock
with its flickering sky
I look up at.

The hairs of Mohammed's beard
are under glass. And his footprint
stays in the stone
where he flew to heaven.

I move in a circle on my bare feet
looking for signs, one quill
from the wing of the angel
who stopped the knife.

All day my head spins
in a great hollow. Holding it up.

20

See that man with the basket
of fruit and vegetables?

You mean by the Roman arch?

The one with the blue shirt
and sandals.

By the Sixth Station of the Cross?

With the child eating a banana.

Where Veronica wiped the sweat
from His face with her handkerchief?

No. No. The blue shirt,
the basket of vegetables.

21

If I go down to the docks
in Seattle where the ferries
are loading for the next trip,
or watch how the lights come on
in their pale fuzz as I'm walking
home through the rain, my mother's still
wiping the dust from the lamp shades
with a damp rag, crying.

If I go down to the Judean desert
where the cliffs line up
on their knees to face the sunrise,
sages come out of their caves
like old lovers with their gematria
and their ancient scrolls
and their promises of redemption.

Less insistent than she is.
Like a dark head bobbing out of the cistern,
refusing to drown.

When I stand on this ridge,
the earth slides helpless
in two directions. There's only
Jerusalem on my left, everyone
climbing over the corpses,
on my right the frozen wilderness,
black goats looking for something green.

II
Histories

Whatever they wanted for their sons
will be wanted forever, success,
the right wife, they should be
good to their mothers.

One day they meet at the rock
where Isaac was cut free
at the last minute. Sarah stands
with her shoes off under the dome
showing the tourists with their Minoltas
around their necks the place
where Mohammed flew up to heaven.
Hagar is on her knees
in the women's section praying.

They bump into each other at the door,
the dark still heavy on their backs
like the future always coming after them.
Sarah wants to find out what happened
to Ishmael but is afraid to ask.
Hagar's lips make a crooked seam
over her accusations.

They know that the world is flat,
and if they move to the edge
they're sure to fall over. They know
they can only follow their own feet
the way they came.
Jet planes fly over their heads

as they walk out of each other's lives
like the last time, silent, not mentioning
the angels of god and the bright
miracles of birth and water. Not telling
that the boys are gone.

The air ticks slowly. It's August
and the heat is sick of itself
waiting all summer for rain.

Sarah is in her cool villa.
She keeps her eyes on the pot
so it won't boil over.
She brings the food to the table
where he's already seated
reading the afternoon paper
or listening to the news,
the common corruptions they don't
even speak about now.
Guess who I met she says talking
across the desert.

Hagar shops in the market.
There's a run on chickens, the grapes
are finished and the plums are soft.
She fills her bag with warm bread
fresh from the oven thinking
there's nothing to forgive,
I got what I wanted

from the old man.
The flight in the wilderness
is a morning stroll.
She buys a kilo of ripe figs. She
climbs the dusty path home.

23   **Stones**

When you live in Jerusalem you begin
to feel the weight of stones.
You begin to know the word
was made stone, not flesh.

They dwell among us. They crawl
up the hillsides and lie down
on each other to build a wall.
They don't care about prayers,
the small slips of paper
we feed them between the cracks.

They stamp at the earth
until the air runs out
and nothing can grow.

They stare at the sun without blinking
and when they've had enough,
make holes in the sky
so the rain will run down their faces.

They sprawl all over the town
with their pitted bodies. They want
to be water, but nobody
strikes them anymore.

Sometimes at night I hear them
licking the wind to drive it crazy.
There's a huge rock lying on my chest
and I can't get up.

24   Relics

Herod's bath house flakes
in the sun and the round stones
stay where the Romans hurled them,
ballista wound like a clock and suddenly
released
on roofs on walls astonished faces.

Like snowballs rolled in a negative of winter,
balls I played with on the beach at Alki
or poured my breath into
watching the skin stretch,
globes with the map of the world
turned black.

There are no trees here
and when the sun goes down
nothing holds on to it.

The last light slips
into somebody else's day.

Cabbages and beans
where the flood waters poured
from the Temple Mount
into the Kidron valley.

The pool of Siloam
a trickle of water in the mud.

The archaeologist is speaking about millenia.
He shows us what's left of the city
that David took—the edge of a tower.
The Jebusites gathered their crippled
and their blind, leaned them like scarecrows
on the wall.

We look at the hill
to find the level where they stand
as if the air still passes
through their sleeves.

Forty—one contestants in the seventh annual
International Harp Contest are trying out
at the Jerusalem Y.M.C.A. The lecture
goes on in the next room.

Sheep in the City of David.

They move in their dumb heaviness
past the houses where the boy leads them
into the field. Past the dim little crèche
and the candles eating their hearts out
in soft puddles of wax.

Like the wick that runs out of itself.
The plucking of strings.

Now the king has a headache.
We lean back together,
waiting for the music to begin.

27   Abishag

*...and let her lie in thy bosom that the lord my king
may get heat.*

I Kings 1:2

That's what they ordered
for the old man
to dangle around his neck,
send currents of fever
through his phlegmatic nerves, something
like rabbit fur, silky,
or maybe a goat—hair blanket
to tickle his chin.

He can do nothing else
but wear her, pluck at her body
like a lost bird
pecking in winter.
He spreads her out
like a road—map, trying
to find his way from one point
to another, unable.

She thinks if she pinches
his hand it will turn to powder.
She feels his thin claws, his wings
spread over her like arms, not bones
but feathers ready to fall.
She suffers the jerk

of his feeble legs. Take it easy,
she tells him, cruelly

submissive in her bright flesh.
He's cold from the fear
of death, the sorrow
of failure, night after night
he shivers with her breasts
against him like an accusation,
her mouth slightly open,
her hair spilling everywhere.

28

History is what we choose
to remember, peeling the present
from its skin like a ripe orange,
juice on our fingers.

Or the mist slipping over
my father where he lies
in one half of his body
unable to speak.

Trying to find the way
is like reading a street sign
in the distance, the letters
blurred and unfocused
until I come closer.

And then I discover
it's only a marker at the border
saying STOP.

29   **Between wars**

Our friends are sorting
the clothes of their son.
What a brown heap of cotton
for the lost shape.

Everything's closed
like the well in the courtyard
with its slimy film,
wide mouth of longing
under the lid.

Or the cemetery crowded with beds
the dead lie under.

He was killed between wars, between
our line and their line,
a forest of wire.

We put rocks on his grave
to weigh him down
when his spirit gets restless.

30   Sheep

All morning they've been rounding up
the sheep so they can strip the wool
from their bleeding skins.

Child—bride faces. They run
in the yard shaved naked
not knowing who they are.

If all the exiled of the earth,
speech failing, hands losing touch,
would say what I have no right to—
having no calling, not even for hunger—

if all the strangers I know as myself now
not quite belonging would begin to speak
over the bleating and the slice of shears

their words would fall
lighter than snowflakes, little flags
of surrender to the dead.

As the reel turns

At ten the siren warns us to stop
what we are doing and remember the dead
whom nobody warns.

They are not listening.
They could be nodding there forever
in Lvov, Vilna, Bialystock, plucking
their kosher chickens, dealing
in second–hand pants or salt herring.
It is the summer of 1939.

All those couples strolling as the reel turns
in the gardens of the Duke's palace,
blinking in the strong light.

All those children stretched out at rest time
on the lawn of the Workers' Summer Camp
with their sticky fingers.

A man sleeps on a bench in the park
as if he owned it, as if
he might wake up out of the movie
opulent in California.

There are lace curtains in the windows
of Dr. Zamenhof's house
through which the sun cuts holes
in the universal language.

A woman arranges the blanket
over her baby in the carriage.
How careful she is
to get the edges straight.

32   Uncles

When they take off their shoes
their pale feet fall from the picture
into mass graves.

Uncle Max has just come from the barber
with his moustache trimmed.
Leib makes a face.
His eyes are my mother's forgetting
the eyes of uncles,
little brown ghosts from Poland
in strange clothes.

I want to close the mouth
of Mokka on the left
with his gold teeth missing.

33   Saving the whales

The visitor from Boston
sits on our balcony facing the Valley
of the Cross, drinking iced tea.
We tell her about the monastery
and the tree. She is moist
with compassion. She is saving
the whales, she says,
and nobody cares.

I move so little in the midday heat
to keep my blood quiet, to keep it
from sweating through my skin,
I may not exist. What
can I say about salvation?

Three spoons of sugar
and a sprig of mint.
Her sips are so small
I can't even hear them go down.

White moon even by day.
It should know better,
balancing sideways like a moth
that can't stay out of the light.

We're leaning over the valley
where the dead lie
stacked on each other
waiting to rise. I want
to be down there with them
when the time comes, all of us
talking at once and slightly embarrassed,
pumping our muscles through the new flesh,
jiggling our wings.

Strange—what they tell us
now, the ones who have died
for a minute and come back,
hooked to machines and bottles.
They recall how the world
dropped off the sill into
daylight, how they hovered
a little above their last breath
while their eyes were fixed
on a dazzling point in the distance,
bright gleam on the water
like a prize held out to an infant
learning to walk.

One light is as good as another,
desire transforms us
to the end. Still I'd like to believe
they saw what my grandfather
prayed for.

When I was a child my mother
took me to his synagogue
on the most holy day. We climbed
to the women's gallery, so hot
in Indian summer, bodies
buttoned up and weak from fasting,
somebody always fainted.
Grandma held a vial of ammonia
in her blue–veined hand

and poured some into her hankie,
sniffing it up her nose.
Fasting and fainting, I knew then
that God was too much for me.

Sometimes at dusk I watch
the devoted at the Western Wall
who jerk their shoulders, sway
and bow, ecstatic and blind.

And there's an old man on Jaffa Road
who sits on the sidewalk selling
prayers. All day he squats
in his rags against the storefront,
holding out little blessings
on pieces of paper.

I've run from a flock of elders
through my whole life, fidgety
sparrows dropping crumbs
from their small beaks
to show the lost children
the way through the forest.

By what fervor, nailed
on our doorposts, worn as a sign
between the eyes, can we
manage our lives?
By what diligence of faith
give them up?

36   Fawn

The fawn we rescued on the road
to Nes Harim where dogs
had cornered it, its mother gone,
refuses the bottled milk,

refuses the logic of our hands.
The smallest offer makes it
tremble on skinny legs
that barely stand.

It is trying to keep
its bones together, the ponds
of its eyes won't focus.
They reflect nothing.
It is too soon.

Stroke the head, the silky
place between the ears.

We can only invent
what we think it needs.

37   Isolation

In the hospital on Mount Scopus
the woman in the next bed
keeps her eyes closed
and cries to herself to release
her body. No one can lift her
when she tries to rearrange her grief.
And when she moans, the pain pulls her
inside where I can't follow.

All night she called for someone
to hear her, names of the dead
she said as if they were there
in the dark, unwilling to answer.

Now her daughter plucks the hairs
from her chin with a tweezer
and she tells her the nurses
never come.

*

None of them. Even our mothers
under the green lawns
where they forget how deaf they are.

Angel over my head in the old life:
I'm thirsty or I'm hot
there's a mosquito
the radio's too loud.

They stand in the doorway
for the last time, soft
and bewildered, and we know
we'll leave them entirely
to themselves.

★

When I was five at Mrs. Tarlow's
I threw up because she forced me
to eat boiled carrots, and once
she made me stand in the closet.

I wasn't afraid of the dark,
there were things that glittered,
but the silence—
they would all forget me
and go home. I screamed
till I lost my breath
and they let me into the kind world.

★

The woman is beating the pillow
with her head. She will not
take what they promise.
Her head is a black scarf
tied to the end of a stick.
When I speak, it's not in her language

so I offer her mildness
which she refuses as she refuses
meat in the hospital gravy.

They are smoothing the pillows,
removing the wilted flowers, drawing
the curtain between our beds.

Food spoils in this endless summer
faster than we can eat it
but we sniff at the meat
because we can't be sure.

When a bomb exploded
in the mail box, they narrowed
the slots. Only
one letter at a time.

We are learning distrust.
Our neighor cut down the pine tree
when we were out because it blocked
his light and the roots were splitting
the side of his house.
There is his window
where the branch should be.

My old self is lying in the grass
where the tree was,
watching my breath move
slowly between the blades.

I try to get into it again
like a cold foot pulling on its sock.

39   After so little

It might have been a sister,
mother told me, after she'd let
the seams out over her
thin waist, having to
sew them up again.

She grew so pure in her grieving
she no longer saw the blood.

Hunger forgets what it came for
when the fingers won't tighten
around the spoon and food
is sawdust in the reluctant mouth,

chewing and chewing what I fed her,
refusing to swallow
the lump on her tongue.

Her hands with their shiny knuckles
are lighter than anything she held.

They are obsequious as aliens,
swabbed clean, exiled
even under the ground.

★

After so little to be used up.
Her body couldn't unlearn
its emptiness.

Each day the river of tears
dries in its salt
and the salt beds crack in the sun.
Rachel lies in a dream of water
near Bethlehem, slapping the flies.

I won't go inside to that oversized
concrete block with the gilt fringed scarf
they say is her tomb.

Mother lies in my own dream
as the light gets smaller
between her pains.

I help her to squat. The mouth
of my sister strains
to cry out in her first voice,
her breath gets lost
in the unborn throat.

Her hand's on her neck
across the pale seam
where they slit her flesh
to remove the goiter.
So much to forgive
she didn't know how.

Rain wrinkles the glass,
a scrim of water we can't see through.
It's always between us.

She said *you're your father's daughter*
when she looked for excuses.

He hid her in the drawer
when he married another, the photograph
with the dark silk making a long V
down to the center of her breasts

to stop her from watching over the bed
with her stunned eyes.

Now I am no one's daughter.
Rain at the window,
my hand on my neck.

III
Small Comforts

41   Spring

And red poppies.
And after the flower—spattered hills
the Dead Sea. Sunlight
peeling off the old skin.

Not wondering how it happened.
So that the surface floats
on its warm back, smiling.

So that the body loosens itself
to kindness. The one thing
we're ready for.

42

Walking across the park in April
when the blossoms were out
you told me you felt so young again you wanted
to take my hand and swing it
running away at fifty falling in love
you said yes falling because the plunge
begins in heaven with the angels
falling they hold us under their wings
to break the fall.

43

I tell you what I remember
as we climb the uneven terrace,
vineyards they never dreamed of
washed away. How I left them
and left their expectations
and left again.

The first time you brought me
to these eroded hillsides
and we drove past the rush
of silver in the pines,
I wouldn't believe
it was sewage from the town.

Sometimes when you're working
in your room, I stand in the doorway
just to know you are there.

44   Your hands

No one can cut such a perfect
thin slice of Edam for my toast.

At breakfast we sit by the east window
listening to the seven o'clock news:

another hole dug in the military
graveyard; the price of oil.

The sun eases over
your shoulders, your durable hands.

45

Love, when you hold me
nothing is reducible to meaning.

The caves
that open their dark mouths
out of the cliffs
have revealed their secrets
and their secrets are only bones
as we are.

We see by the light of them
in the dark
as they grow luminous again.

I feel them silencing each thought
that perjures itself in words.

When asked for a sample of his work
Giotto took a red pencil,
drew a perfect circle
free hand
and sent it to the Pope.

What does it mean
to be that sure of anything?
The dream of completion.
We cross the field
with the small stones biting our sandals,
picking up shards.

Sometimes you finish
what I think I've said.

We take the clay fragments,
skin—colored, bits of them worn
or crumbling between our fingers,
and piece them together.
Something is always missing.

47

Jan and Miriam are leaving.
His cousin was killed in the last war.
She cradles their month—old baby in her arms
like a half—remembered doll
she never let go of.
His small hand fastens over her finger,
his mouth fastens over her breast,
a homely grip like ivy on the walls.

They want to go back
to their mothers, to live
on a boat drifting in the cool canals
that pass through the green of childhood
without change. To follow
the water where it takes them
away from electrified fences,

the sky all leafy and cordial
and what they imagine.

48   Chosen

Leaves are the color of burned—out
tanks on the road to Jerusalem. Obsolete
armor. Grapes in the market
already smell of wine,
and the flies tap sugar
from their overstuffed skins.

We think we can smell the rain too,
smashing its tiny mirrors in the north
as if what we waited for
might come.

Chosen for what? The live carp
flap in their vats. They think
they should be flying.
I take one home in a plastic bag.

Day of Atonement and the long walk
at sundown to the Wall.
What the sun does to itself,
beating its chest all day,
is already forgotten,
and the goat has gone out
of the Dung Gate with our sins.

The old man lifts his *shofar*
toward the gates of heaven,
blowing the notes to swing them wide
for the last time
before they are bolted for another year.

Now all our days
are measured in the book
against our repentance.

That's a small comfort.
A prayer is not a bird.

50   The Promised Land

. . . and thou shalt be called by a new name . . .
Isaiah 62:2

On your side the license plates
are yellow. On their side blue.

Because of the green line.

Where?

There. The occupied territories.
Judea and Samaria. The West Bank.

You're pointing to houses.

They're over the line.

What line?

The line on the map.

Who drew it?

Now or then?

We get down on the floor at first
because the kittens are there
and it's easy to play with them.
Fierce little faces. Sakhar
shows me her favorite,
lifting its chin.

Where can it lead? From her home
in this Arab city, her taut friends
over the teacups. The color
of license plates tells us
who we are.

I might have stayed
on my own side where it's common
to say the wrong things
and be forgiven.

It's not just a matter of truth
or occupation.
We each have our fables,
the sweet cakes
stick to our fingers as we speak.

The kittens roll over
and the mother finds them,
nursing one hunger at a time.

52

As it gets late
we can't depend on the stars.

If I tell you
today's the Sabbath
then it's Saturday unless it's Friday
and it's your turn to sleep
late in the morning or to pray,
unless it's Sunday and the bells are ringing.

If you tell me
the soul is a lame dog
thrashing its tail, one ear
for the world's contagions, one
for the master with his own versions,

and if we tug at this city
in our blindfolds
until it splits and goes
sailing over the mountains,

what will become of your fast days
and my atonement, what
will become of us?

53   After the wars

The widows forget nothing.
When they open a window, the wind
is the breath of their anger
knocking things over.

The bare stones blind them.
If they close their eyes
a dark space enters. They keep it
under their eyelids when they sleep.

In the morning the space
surprises them in their beds.
It stands in the mirror
while they brush their hair.

At home after work
they prepare the meal. They serve
the cold soup at the table.
The space is there.

Even when they take off
their black scarves. Even
when the children grow up.
They are not consoled.

The widows forget nothing.
It's no good telling them
that their loss
is everyone's loss.

This curve of the pitcher,
thrust of the handle against my palm,
this lip where I run
my finger over the edge
has no regard for function
or for thirst.
And what if it leaks?

The imperfect body
in its worn—out skin.

Salim can fix it. Thirty years
in his shop in the Old City
polishing pots and skillets
in their sour grease, kettles and pans.
For his brother to change
to *dinars* in Amman.

He makes it shine. As his face
shines out of its paler glaze.
He holds a tin stick in the flame
until the drops form,
white—hot and glassy,
sealing the pitcher with a scab.

This is our bond. This mending,
over the wreckage on his floor.
He smooths the excess
and the gleam of copper
mirrors our hands.

55

Jerusalem is a plank of cedar, lashed
to another, beached on sand spit
waiting for the tide.

The sea rises swiftly,
lots of deep water,
and we scramble on.

So full of splinters,
so little room,
sharks, strong currents,
and so forth.

When it gets dark
they turn on the Sound and Light show
and let us drown.

But this is a life raft!
somebody cries.

Yes. Yes. That was the idea.

56

Jerusalem is a melon
You tap it, inhale it,
push your finger in the rind
when the man isn't looking
to see if it's soft but not rotten.
And still you're not sure.

When you slice it in half,
the seeds fall out
of the little pink tub in the center
and it smells like Solomon's temple.

So you eat it.

57   **Roots in the air**

Over my head
the Bengal ficus
dangles its roots like seaweed
out of the sea, licking
the ashes from the air.

Sure of which way is down
but unable to get there,
one tree makes a hundred
out of the steaming soil it comes from,
replanting itself.

Not here,
The roots are shaggy
with trying in this land.
No earth, no water,
what are they doing
in the light?

58   The order of things

I am digging a hole
for the family tree, shovelling
this lumpy earth of yearning
out of the bed rock
to make room.

I pack my life hard around it,
the part I let go of, apples
and kisses where my cousin instructed me
under our tree and climbed
for the ripest apples at the top.
I didn't dare to shinny up that high.

Rabbi ben Zakkai said: If there's a tree
in your hand when they tell you
Behold the Messiah!
first plant the tree
and afterwards go out to greet him.

That's why olive trees
in the garden of Gethsemane
are as old as Christ.

59   Levitation

All heaven to choose from
and the starlings are thinning themselves
to smoke screens heading south.
The season is late, the trees
have lost track of the time
hanging on to their frail leaves,
and the long dry summer still
stiffens the ground.

The future is here. It already
regrets what hasn't begun to happen.

What did I think would happen?
I lie here dreaming of levitation.
Maybe you'll bring me
a bowl of rice in mid-air.
I need to be held to the light
like the blue glass of Hebron
through which the sun streams.
I need to be raised up
like a roof the dawn discovers
with the sky crouched over it.

The sky leans on its elbows
smiling. There is more of it
than earth, than anything.

There are long roots everywhere
cracking the stone foundations,
drinking the secret rivers underground.
Great forests wanting to be born.

Once on a summer day in Auvers
I found Van Gogh's room,
climbed the steep staircase to the door,
the metal bed against the wall, the chair
with its straw seat brown as sorrow,
and the narrow unwashed window
like the space between two bars in a cell.
No light came through.
How it was anything but yellow.

We make what we can
of things as they are, in praise
of our bodies on the bed.

Bright heave of the waves
in this waterless city.
This blazing sun.

61

Trees find their shapes again,
as the world blanches. It must be morning.

At the window I can make out the dim outlines
of the domes the towers lit by the dawn.

On the sill the dove sleeps
over her two damp birds.
She built a nest in the pot of geraniums
and yesterday they hatched,
little homemade bombs.
They are not Jews or Arabs.

62   Autumn crocus

I go to the center of the world
near the edge of Jerusalem
where the grapes are all picked
and the men are climbing
into the olive trees.

I watch how they beat the branches
and the dark fruit drops to the ground.
The families move in and out
of the dust to gather them.

October again.
The rains are coming, the steep cold
and the festering idleness.

The women are sorting the bitter crop.
In the empty fields small
clusters of lavender petals
explode from the soil
without any warning, not even
a stem or a single leaf.
A kind of privilege. As if
they earned the right
through the exacting summer.

Look! They say for a moment.